TRUCKING

I0201934

SAVE MONEY
ON THE ROAD
TRUCKING EXPENSE SHEET

JESSE BUTLER

Interior design and layout by Jesse Butler,
Text copyright © 2018 by Jesse Butler, Publishing Our Children's Stories.
Design and cover copyright © 2018 by Jesse Butler
All rights reserved. No part of this book may be reproduced in any form or
by any electronic or mechanical means including information storage and
retrieval systems-except in the case of brief quotations embodied in critical
articles or reviews-without permission in writing from its publisher,
Jesse Butler.

Published by Jesse Butler.
Great Falls, MT 59404
(406) 356-6116

ISBN 978-0-9997444-0-6

MONTHLY FIXED EXPENSES

MONTH

EXPENSE   AMOUNT

TOTAL MONTHLY EXPENSES

AMOUNT TOWARDS SAVINGS

AMOUNT TOWARDS GIVING

Now, let's track your expenses for accuracy. Know where your money is going is key.

DAILY EXPENSES

DATE

DAILY LOAD #

PAID MILES

PAY PER MILE X PAID MILES

EXTRA PAYS (DETENTION, LAYOVER,
BREAKDOWN, EXTRA DROP & PICK
WASHOUTS, ETC.

EXPECTED DAILY EARNINGS

PURCHASE	AMOUNT

TOTAL PURCHASES FOR THE DATE

DAILY EXPENSES

DATE

DAILY LOAD #

PAID MILES

PAY PER MILE X PAID MILES

EXTRA PAYS (DETENTION, LAYOVER,
BREAKDOWN, EXTRA DROP & PICK
WASHOUTS, ETC.

EXPECTED DAILY EARNINGS

PURCHASE   AMOUNT

TOTAL PURCHASES FOR THE DATE

DAILY EXPENSES

DATE

DAILY LOAD #

PAID MILES

PAY PER MILE X PAID MILES

EXTRA PAYS (DETENTION, LAYOVER,
BREAKDOWN, EXTRA DROP & PICK
WASHOUTS, ETC.

EXPECTED DAILY EARNINGS

PURCHASE   AMOUNT

TOTAL PURCHASES FOR THE DATE

DAILY EXPENSES

DATE

DAILY LOAD #

PAID MILES

PAY PER MILE X PAID MILES

EXTRA PAYS (DETENTION, LAYOVER, BREAKDOWN, EXTRA DROP & PICK WASHOUTS, ETC.

EXPECTED DAILY EARNINGS

PURCHASE   AMOUNT

TOTAL PURCHASES FOR THE DATE

DAILY EXPENSES

DATE

DAILY LOAD #

PAID MILES

PAY PER MILE X PAID MILES

EXTRA PAYS (DETENTION, LAYOVER, BREAKDOWN, EXTRA DROP & PICK WASHOUTS, ETC.

EXPECTED DAILY EARNINGS

PURCHASE   AMOUNT

TOTAL PURCHASES FOR THE DATE

DAILY EXPENSES

DATE

DAILY LOAD #

PAID MILES

PAY PER MILE X PAID MILES

EXTRA PAYS (DETENTION, LAYOVER,
BREAKDOWN, EXTRA DROP & PICK
WASHOUTS, ETC.

EXPECTED DAILY EARNINGS

PURCHASE   AMOUNT

TOTAL PURCHASES FOR THE DATE

DAILY EXPENSES

DATE

DAILY LOAD #

PAID MILES

PAY PER MILE X PAID MILES

EXTRA PAYS (DETENTION, LAYOVER,
BREAKDOWN, EXTRA DROP & PICK
WASHOUTS, ETC.

EXPECTED DAILY EARNINGS

PURCHASE   AMOUNT

TOTAL PURCHASES FOR THE DATE

WEEKLY EARNINGS

WEEK OF:

LOAD #

LOAD #

LOAD #

LOAD #

LOAD #

LOAD #

LOAD #

LOAD #

LOAD #

LOAD #

EXTRA PAY AMOUNT/ LOAD #

EXTRA PAY AMOUNT/ LOAD #

EXTRA PAY AMOUNT/ LOAD #

EXTRA PAY AMOUNT/ LOAD #

EXTRA PAY AMOUNT/ LOAD #

EXPECTED WEEKLY EARNINGS

WEEKLY EXPENSES

WEEK OF:

TOTAL PURCHASES FOR MONDAY

TOTAL PURCHASES FOR TUESDAY

TOTAL PURCHASES FOR WEDNESDAY

TOTAL PURCHASES FOR THURSDAY

TOTAL PURCHASES FOR FRIDAY

TOTAL PURCHASES FOR SATURDAY

TOTAL PURCHASES FOR SUNDAY

TOTAL PURCHASES FOR THE WEEK

DAILY EXPENSES

DATE

DAILY LOAD #

PAID MILES

PAY PER MILE X PAID MILES

EXTRA PAYS (DETENTION, LAYOVER,
BREAKDOWN, EXTRA DROP & PICK
WASHOUTS, ETC.

EXPECTED DAILY EARNINGS

PURCHASE   AMOUNT

TOTAL PURCHASES FOR THE DATE

DAILY EXPENSES

DATE

DAILY LOAD #

PAID MILES

PAY PER MILE X PAID MILES

EXTRA PAYS (DETENTION, LAYOVER,
BREAKDOWN, EXTRA DROP & PICK
WASHOUTS, ETC.

EXPECTED DAILY EARNINGS

PURCHASE   AMOUNT

TOTAL PURCHASES FOR THE DATE

DAILY EXPENSES

DATE

DAILY LOAD #

PAID MILES

PAY PER MILE X PAID MILES

EXTRA PAYS (DETENTION, LAYOVER,
BREAKDOWN, EXTRA DROP & PICK
WASHOUTS, ETC.

EXPECTED DAILY EARNINGS

PURCHASE   AMOUNT

TOTAL PURCHASES FOR THE DATE

DAILY EXPENSES

DATE

DAILY LOAD #

PAID MILES

PAY PER MILE X PAID MILES

EXTRA PAYS (DETENTION, LAYOVER, BREAKDOWN, EXTRA DROP & PICK WASHOUTS, ETC.

EXPECTED DAILY EARNINGS

PURCHASE   AMOUNT

TOTAL PURCHASES FOR THE DATE

DAILY EXPENSES

DATE

DAILY LOAD #

PAID MILES

PAY PER MILE X PAID MILES

EXTRA PAYS (DETENTION, LAYOVER,
BREAKDOWN, EXTRA DROP & PICK
WASHOUTS, ETC.

EXPECTED DAILY EARNINGS

PURCHASE   AMOUNT

TOTAL PURCHASES FOR THE DATE

DAILY EXPENSES

DATE

DAILY LOAD #

PAID MILES

PAY PER MILE X PAID MILES

EXTRA PAYS (DETENTION, LAYOVER,
BREAKDOWN, EXTRA DROP & PICK
WASHOUTS, ETC.

EXPECTED DAILY EARNINGS

PURCHASE   AMOUNT

TOTAL PURCHASES FOR THE DATE

DAILY EXPENSES

DATE

DAILY LOAD #

PAID MILES

PAY PER MILE X PAID MILES

EXTRA PAYS (DETENTION, LAYOVER, BREAKDOWN, EXTRA DROP & PICK WASHOUTS, ETC.

EXPECTED DAILY EARNINGS

PURCHASE   AMOUNT

TOTAL PURCHASES FOR THE DATE

WEEKLY EARNINGS

WEEK OF:

LOAD #

LOAD #

LOAD #

LOAD #

LOAD #

LOAD #

LOAD #

LOAD #

LOAD #

LOAD #

LOAD #

EXTRA PAY AMOUNT/ LOAD #

EXTRA PAY AMOUNT/ LOAD #

EXTRA PAY AMOUNT/ LOAD #

EXTRA PAY AMOUNT/ LOAD #

EXTRA PAY AMOUNT/ LOAD #

EXPECTED WEEKLY EARNINGS

WEEKLY EXPENSES

WEEK OF:

TOTAL PURCHASES FOR MONDAY

TOTAL PURCHASES FOR TUESDAY

TOTAL PURCHASES FOR WEDNESDAY

TOTAL PURCHASES FOR THURSDAY

TOTAL PURCHASES FOR FRIDAY

TOTAL PURCHASES FOR SATURDAY

TOTAL PURCHASES FOR SUNDAY

TOTAL PURCHASES FOR THE WEEK

DAILY EXPENSES

DATE

DAILY LOAD #

PAID MILES

PAY PER MILE X PAID MILES

EXTRA PAYS (DETENTION, LAYOVER,
BREAKDOWN, EXTRA DROP & PICK
WASHOUTS, ETC.

EXPECTED DAILY EARNINGS

PURCHASE   AMOUNT

TOTAL PURCHASES FOR THE DATE

DAILY EXPENSES

DATE

DAILY LOAD #

PAID MILES

PAY PER MILE X PAID MILES

EXTRA PAYS (DETENTION, LAYOVER,
BREAKDOWN, EXTRA DROP & PICK
WASHOUTS, ETC.

EXPECTED DAILY EARNINGS

PURCHASE   AMOUNT

TOTAL PURCHASES FOR THE DATE

DAILY EXPENSES

DATE

DAILY LOAD #

PAID MILES

PAY PER MILE X PAID MILES

EXTRA PAYS (DETENTION, LAYOVER,
BREAKDOWN, EXTRA DROP & PICK
WASHOUTS, ETC.

EXPECTED DAILY EARNINGS

PURCHASE	AMOUNT

TOTAL PURCHASES FOR THE DATE

DAILY EXPENSES

DATE

DAILY LOAD #

PAID MILES

PAY PER MILE X PAID MILES

EXTRA PAYS (DETENTION, LAYOVER,
BREAKDOWN, EXTRA DROP & PICK
WASHOUTS, ETC.

EXPECTED DAILY EARNINGS

PURCHASE   AMOUNT

TOTAL PURCHASES FOR THE DATE

DAILY EXPENSES

DATE

DAILY LOAD #

PAID MILES

PAY PER MILE X PAID MILES

EXTRA PAYS (DETENTION, LAYOVER,
BREAKDOWN, EXTRA DROP & PICK
WASHOUTS, ETC.

EXPECTED DAILY EARNINGS

PURCHASE   AMOUNT

TOTAL PURCHASES FOR THE DATE

DAILY EXPENSES

DATE

DAILY LOAD #

PAID MILES

PAY PER MILE X PAID MILES

EXTRA PAYS (DETENTION, LAYOVER,
BREAKDOWN, EXTRA DROP & PICK
WASHOUTS, ETC.

EXPECTED DAILY EARNINGS

PURCHASE   AMOUNT

TOTAL PURCHASES FOR THE DATE

DAILY EXPENSES

DATE

DAILY LOAD #

PAID MILES

PAY PER MILE X PAID MILES

EXTRA PAYS (DETENTION, LAYOVER,
BREAKDOWN, EXTRA DROP & PICK
WASHOUTS, ETC.

EXPECTED DAILY EARNINGS

PURCHASE   AMOUNT

TOTAL PURCHASES FOR THE DATE

WEEKLY EARNINGS

WEEK OF:

LOAD #

LOAD #

LOAD #

LOAD #

LOAD #

LOAD #

LOAD #

LOAD #

LOAD #

LOAD #

LOAD #

EXTRA PAY AMOUNT/ LOAD #

EXTRA PAY AMOUNT/ LOAD #

EXTRA PAY AMOUNT/ LOAD #

EXTRA PAY AMOUNT/ LOAD #

EXTRA PAY AMOUNT/ LOAD #

EXPECTED WEEKLY EARNINGS

WEEKLY EXPENSES

WEEK OF:

TOTAL PURCHASES FOR MONDAY

TOTAL PURCHASES FOR TUESDAY

TOTAL PURCHASES FOR WEDNESDAY

TOTAL PURCHASES FOR THURSDAY

TOTAL PURCHASES FOR FRIDAY

TOTAL PURCHASES FOR SATURDAY

TOTAL PURCHASES FOR SUNDAY

TOTAL PURCHASES FOR THE WEEK

DAILY EXPENSES

DATE

DAILY LOAD #

PAID MILES

PAY PER MILE X PAID MILES

EXTRA PAYS (DETENTION, LAYOVER,
BREAKDOWN, EXTRA DROP & PICK
WASHOUTS, ETC.

EXPECTED DAILY EARNINGS

PURCHASE   AMOUNT

TOTAL PURCHASES FOR THE DATE

DAILY EXPENSES

DATE

DAILY LOAD #

PAID MILES

PAY PER MILE X PAID MILES

EXTRA PAYS (DETENTION, LAYOVER,
BREAKDOWN, EXTRA DROP & PICK
WASHOUTS, ETC.

EXPECTED DAILY EARNINGS

PURCHASE   AMOUNT

TOTAL PURCHASES FOR THE DATE

DAILY EXPENSES

DATE

DAILY LOAD #

PAID MILES

PAY PER MILE X PAID MILES

EXTRA PAYS (DETENTION, LAYOVER,
BREAKDOWN, EXTRA DROP & PICK
WASHOUTS, ETC.

EXPECTED DAILY EARNINGS

PURCHASE   AMOUNT

TOTAL PURCHASES FOR THE DATE

DAILY EXPENSES

DATE

DAILY LOAD #

PAID MILES

PAY PER MILE X PAID MILES

EXTRA PAYS (DETENTION, LAYOVER,
BREAKDOWN, EXTRA DROP & PICK
WASHOUTS, ETC.

EXPECTED DAILY EARNINGS

PURCHASE   AMOUNT

TOTAL PURCHASES FOR THE DATE

DAILY EXPENSES

DATE

DAILY LOAD #

PAID MILES

PAY PER MILE X PAID MILES

EXTRA PAYS (DETENTION, LAYOVER,
BREAKDOWN, EXTRA DROP & PICK
WASHOUTS, ETC.

EXPECTED DAILY EARNINGS

PURCHASE   AMOUNT

TOTAL PURCHASES FOR THE DATE

DAILY EXPENSES

DATE

DAILY LOAD #

PAID MILES

PAY PER MILE X PAID MILES

EXTRA PAYS (DETENTION, LAYOVER,
BREAKDOWN, EXTRA DROP & PICK
WASHOUTS, ETC.

EXPECTED DAILY EARNINGS

PURCHASE   AMOUNT

TOTAL PURCHASES FOR THE DATE

DAILY EXPENSES

DATE

DAILY LOAD #

PAID MILES

PAY PER MILE X PAID MILES

EXTRA PAYS (DETENTION, LAYOVER,
BREAKDOWN, EXTRA DROP & PICK
WASHOUTS, ETC.

EXPECTED DAILY EARNINGS

PURCHASE   AMOUNT

TOTAL PURCHASES FOR THE DATE

WEEKLY EARNINGS

WEEK OF:

LOAD #

LOAD #

LOAD #

LOAD #

LOAD #

LOAD #

LOAD #

LOAD #

LOAD #

LOAD #

LOAD #

EXTRA PAY AMOUNT/ LOAD #

EXTRA PAY AMOUNT/ LOAD #

EXTRA PAY AMOUNT/ LOAD #

EXTRA PAY AMOUNT/ LOAD #

EXTRA PAY AMOUNT/ LOAD #

EXPECTED WEEKLY EARNINGS

WEEKLY EXPENSES

WEEK OF:

TOTAL PURCHASES FOR MONDAY

TOTAL PURCHASES FOR TUESDAY

TOTAL PURCHASES FOR WEDNESDAY

TOTAL PURCHASES FOR THURSDAY

TOTAL PURCHASES FOR FRIDAY

TOTAL PURCHASES FOR SATURDAY

TOTAL PURCHASES FOR SUNDAY

TOTAL PURCHASES FOR THE WEEK

DAILY EXPENSES

DATE

DAILY LOAD #

PAID MILES

PAY PER MILE X PAID MILES

EXTRA PAYS (DETENTION, LAYOVER, BREAKDOWN, EXTRA DROP & PICK WASHOUTS, ETC.

EXPECTED DAILY EARNINGS

PURCHASE   AMOUNT

TOTAL PURCHASES FOR THE DATE

DAILY EXPENSES

DATE

DAILY LOAD #

PAID MILES

PAY PER MILE X PAID MILES

EXTRA PAYS (DETENTION, LAYOVER,
BREAKDOWN, EXTRA DROP & PICK
WASHOUTS, ETC.

EXPECTED DAILY EARNINGS

PURCHASE	AMOUNT

TOTAL PURCHASES FOR THE DATE

DAILY EXPENSES

DATE

DAILY LOAD #

PAID MILES

PAY PER MILE X PAID MILES

EXTRA PAYS (DETENTION, LAYOVER,
BREAKDOWN, EXTRA DROP & PICK
WASHOUTS, ETC.

EXPECTED DAILY EARNINGS

PURCHASE   AMOUNT

TOTAL PURCHASES FOR THE DATE

DAILY EXPENSES

DATE

DAILY LOAD #

PAID MILES

PAY PER MILE X PAID MILES

EXTRA PAYS (DETENTION, LAYOVER,
BREAKDOWN, EXTRA DROP & PICK
WASHOUTS, ETC.

EXPECTED DAILY EARNINGS

PURCHASE   AMOUNT

TOTAL PURCHASES FOR THE DATE

DAILY EXPENSES

DATE

DAILY LOAD #

PAID MILES

PAY PER MILE X PAID MILES

EXTRA PAYS (DETENTION, LAYOVER,
BREAKDOWN, EXTRA DROP & PICK
WASHOUTS, ETC.

EXPECTED DAILY EARNINGS

PURCHASE   AMOUNT

TOTAL PURCHASES FOR THE DATE

DAILY EXPENSES

DATE

DAILY LOAD #

PAID MILES

PAY PER MILE X PAID MILES

EXTRA PAYS (DETENTION, LAYOVER,
BREAKDOWN, EXTRA DROP & PICK
WASHOUTS, ETC.

EXPECTED DAILY EARNINGS

PURCHASE   AMOUNT

TOTAL PURCHASES FOR THE DATE

DAILY EXPENSES

DATE

DAILY LOAD #

PAID MILES

PAY PER MILE X PAID MILES

EXTRA PAYS (DETENTION, LAYOVER,
BREAKDOWN, EXTRA DROP & PICK
WASHOUTS, ETC.

EXPECTED DAILY EARNINGS

PURCHASE	AMOUNT

TOTAL PURCHASES FOR THE DATE

WEEKLY EARNINGS

WEEK OF:

LOAD #

LOAD #

LOAD #

LOAD #

LOAD #

LOAD #

LOAD #

LOAD #

LOAD #

LOAD #

LOAD #

EXTRA PAY AMOUNT/ LOAD #

EXTRA PAY AMOUNT/ LOAD #

EXTRA PAY AMOUNT/ LOAD #

EXTRA PAY AMOUNT/ LOAD #

EXTRA PAY AMOUNT/ LOAD #

EXPECTED WEEKLY EARNINGS

WEEKLY EXPENSES

WEEK OF:

TOTAL PURCHASES FOR MONDAY

TOTAL PURCHASES FOR TUESDAY

TOTAL PURCHASES FOR WEDNESDAY

TOTAL PURCHASES FOR THURSDAY

TOTAL PURCHASES FOR FRIDAY

TOTAL PURCHASES FOR SATURDAY

TOTAL PURCHASES FOR SUNDAY

TOTAL PURCHASES FOR THE WEEK

END OF MONTH

MONTH

TOTAL PURCHASES FOR THE WEEK: _____

CHECK AMOUNT FOR THE WEEK: _____

TOTAL PURCHASES FOR THE WEEK: _____

CHECK AMOUNT FOR THE WEEK: _____

TOTAL PURCHASES FOR THE WEEK: _____

CHECK AMOUNT FOR THE WEEK: _____

TOTAL PURCHASES FOR THE WEEK: _____

CHECK AMOUNT FOR THE WEEK: _____

TOTAL PURCHASES FOR THE WEEK: _____

CHECK AMOUNT FOR THE WEEK: _____

TOTAL PURCHASES FOR THE MONTH:

_____

TOTAL MONTHLY FIXED EXPENSES

_____

TOTAL MONTHLY CHECKS:

_____

EARNINGS REMAINING

Monthly Checks Totaled - Total Expenses = Remaining
Earnings Calculated
To go toward savings

REVIEW YOUR EXPENSES

Can you put more into savings?
Can you put more into 401K?
Do you need to cut back on expenses out on the road?
Do you need to cut back on expenses at home or during home time?
Can you do a better job of managing your time to help increase drive time availability?
Are you taking cash advances? STOP

List areas from your **Daily Expenses** you can reduce:

List areas from your **Monthly Expenses** you can reduce:

SUGGESTIONS

- **AVOID** unnecessary expenses.
- **Purchase food items in bulk at grocery stores or super stores instead of individually at truck stops where they are usually more expensive.**
- **Plan your meals and snacks a week in advance so you are not spending money at every stop.**
- **Make a budget and break it down into amounts to automatically transfer each week into savings accounts for monthly, quarterly, yearly expenses so they don't creep up on you.**

REDUCE TAXABLE INCOME

- **Not every week will be a 3000 mile week, try and put money aside for an emergency fund. (ex: $.05/mile until 3+ months of expenses can be covered if need be)**
- **Listen to Dave Ramsey's podcast for peak financial fitness.**
- **Avoid cash advances.**
- **Take advantage of the fridge and APUs**

PLAN YOUR MEALS

- Be sure to claim the appropriate amount on your federal and state taxes. Many people claim too much and then get less take home each week because of it.
- Reduce taxable income by putting more into your 401K versus sending to the IRS.
- Track your spending.
- Turn in all your paperwork / documents as the load delivers to assure getting paid for the load on time.
- Keep a log of advances (if you MUST get them)

STICK TO A BUDGET

TRACK YOUR PURCHASES

DON'T FORGET NEXT MONTH'S EXPSENSE TRACKING WORK-BOOK

www.ingramcontent.com/pod-product-compliance
Lightning Source LLC
Chambersburg PA
CBHW071936020426

42331CB00010B/2898